AF266257

Watermarks and Tears

Poems for the Journey

Natasha Roblin

Copyright © 2022 Natasha Roblin

Watermarks and Tears
Poems for the Journey
By Natasha Roblin

Self Published By; Natasha Roblin
Website:https://www.facebook.com/soulperchbook

All rights reserved
No part of this book may be reproduced, or stored in a retrieval system, or transmitted
in any form or by any means, electronic, mechanical, photocopying, recording, or
otherwise, without express written permission of the publisher. For permission, contact
Natasha Roblin at soulperchbook@hotmail.com

ISBN-13: 978-0-9958832-3-9

Cover photo by: Gaspar Zaldo image from upsplash.com
Hymns, bible passages and quotes attributed to their authors
Printed in the United States of America

I dedicate this book to God. Let every word bring you glory and honour.
I also dedicate it to every person who feels like it's too late or too dark or too far.
"Where can I go to escape Your Spirit? Where can I flee from Your presence? If I ascend to the heavens, You are there; if I make my bed in Sheol, You are there." -Psalm 139:7-8

"Imagine yourself as a living house. God comes in to rebuild that house. At first, perhaps, you can understand what He is doing. He is getting the drains right and stopping the leaks in the roof and so on; you knew that those jobs needed doing and so you are not surprised. But presently He starts knocking the house about in a way that hurts abominably and does not seem to make any sense. What on earth is He up to? The explanation is that He is building quite a different house from the one you thought of - throwing out a new wing here, putting on an extra floor there, running up towers, making courtyards. You thought you were being made into a decent little cottage: but He is building a palace. He intends to come and live in it Himself."

— C.S. LEWIS

Contents

Prologue

There is a quote that I have heard about art and what good art is. " Art should disturb the comforted and comfort the disturbed " - Cesar A Cruz. That quote has always stayed with me.

So, whether this book comforts or disturbs you, I pray it leads you closer to Jesus. I pray that you see his grace throughout these pages. That God's goodness knocks you over as you read. It's been a journey, but in every moment, God has been leading and guiding and helping me to become who he always wanted me to be.

As you read my words, I pray that you find hope on your journey with Jesus. I hope you hear me saying: I've been there too. Hold on, hold on. The dark doesn't last. Keep going. God loves you. Keep going. We need you!

I separated this book into sections. Each section has poems that are around a particular subject. In addition, each selection of poetry has a hymn that showcases what the poems in that section are on.

These poems are not new. I wrote them years ago, many, many years ago. For me, this book is a placeholder for an exceptionally long season of healing. It's not the ending of my journey, just a different chapter with a different focus. I'm not in the place I was when I wrote these.

Section One

Fanny Crosby - Dark is the Night - Hymn

"1. Dark is the night, and cold the wind is blowing,
Nearer and nearer comes the breakers' roar;
Where shall I go, or whither fly for refuge?
Hide me, my Father, till the storm is o'er.
Refrain
With His loving hand to guide, let the clouds above me
roll,
And the billows in their fury dash around me.
I can brave the wildest storm, with His glory in my soul,
I can sing amidst the tempest—Praise the Lord!
2. Dark is the night, but cheering is the promise,
He will go with me o'er the troubled wave;
Safe He will lead me through the pathless waters,
Jesus, the mighty One, and strong to save. [Refrain]
3. Dark is the night, but lo! the day is breaking,
Onward my bark, unfurl thy every sail,
Now at the helm I see my Father standing,
Soon will my anchor drop within the veil. [Refrain]"

Nights

In the night, I lay here
Curved like a tree
In the night
The storm comes
The wind around me
Reminding me of memories
Buried deep inside
I'm shaking, cracking, quaking
Terror comes to call
It builds itself a treehouse that's sound within my walls
Night after night
I can't take this anymore
I don't have a way to fight this
I need a miracle
Fear and exhaustion do battle over me
Squirrels trying to win a burrow
In this broken tree
Deep in the night
Fear always seems to win
Exhaustion just lays there and eventually digs her heels in
Fear and terror don't seem to care how tired I am
Rock a bye, baby, in my treetop
Sing a lullaby
But the wind doesn't stop

The bough shattered long ago
Broken at the root
Lord, cut me down or help me
I don't have another way
Show up in the darkness
Walk with me through this pain
Dawn seems so far away
Can't find my way to the light
Seems like terror has stolen all my nights

Fire and Ice

Like shades of shattered glass left upon the sea,
Like ice that cuts and fire that burns,
I am drowning in the deep
Can you not see me?
I'm crawling though my heart gives way. I'm fighting for
my breath
Every moment has been this
Since you have left,
I thought you wanted me, just me
You've left me here to die
Amid the shattered shards of ice Chipped way from round
my heart
Until I took your hand in mine
Believed your every word
That you would stay with me
Until the earth gave way
Yet here I am, consumed in fire and ice, Trying to remove
the burns and shards I've built around my heart
Trying to believe that there will come a day
When I can be thankful
Thankful for this pain
I guess I'll stand again
I'm just not sure how to mend
All I know is fire and ice are my constant friends

Fog

Fog
A fog so thick you could slice it
If only a knife could cut it
It wraps its self around me
Tighter and tighter now
Like an octopus crushing its prey,
But I've found it's not a beast
That I can fight or hunt
I don't know how to break free from this one
I've not moved to London I didn't go looking for you
I'm here where I've always been
How did this happen?
I'm not quite sure
How did I get here? And how do I ever get unfurled?
I've never been this deep before
I can't find my way to the light
I don't even know how I got into this
It seemed to sneak in when I couldn't fight
I could see
Until I couldn't
The curtains closed so fast
I've fallen down a deep dark hole
I think that hole was me
Maybe I just never knew
The haze went this deep

I can't feel a thing
Fog, Will you please tell where I am?
Tell me,
How did you come to be?
When will you leave me?
Fog, tell me!
You've gotten quite a lot of me
Do you want the rest?
Will you tell me what your name is?
How I can divest?
Will you clear away someday?
Will you let me think?
Tell me, tell me, tell me, please
What do you want with me?
My mind so deep in the mist
I cannot find my eyes
Tell me what your name is
Tell me why you're in my mind
Tell me how I got here
Tell me you'll not return
Tell me I can finally feel
Tell me fog! oh, tell me
Or let me just pretend
Your tentacles pull me deeper
Is this the end?
If I never wake again,
Tell them that I sleep
In the clouds is where I am
Tucked in deep

Section Two

I Must Tell Jesus- Elisha Hoffman- Hymn

"1 I must tell Jesus all of my trials; I cannot bear these burdens alone; In my distress He kindly will help me; He ever loves and cares for His own.Refrain: I must tell Jesus! I must tell Jesus! I cannot bear my burdens alone; I must tell Jesus! I must tell Jesus! Jesus can help me, Jesus alone.2 I must tell Jesus all of my troubles; He is a kind, compassionate friend; If I but ask Him, He will deliver, Make of my troubles quickly an end. [Refrain] 3 Tempted and tried, I need a great Savior, One who can help my burdens to bear; I must tell Jesus, I must tell Jesus; He all my cares and sorrows will share. [Refrain] 4 O how the world to evil allures me! O how my heart is tempted to sin! I must tell Jesus, and He will help me Over the world the vict'ry to win. [Refrain]"

The Voice of Silent Tears

My voice you took away
Locked it in a cage
Placed inside my rage
Cut off your ears, soundproofed hearts
Poking me with sticks
Pulling from me anything left
Okay, take my voice away
Lock me up with rage
Steal the words
Until I forget
That my voice ever did
Sound
Out loud
Until my voice forgets
How to speak
Questions every syllable
So I learn to fear it
When you let me out
Don't use it
Just turn it into open invitations
For everyone to take
I'm a buffet
Take what you want
Leave the rest
Behind!

With the voice, you left confined
In that cage
Tears silent
Are voices of the voiceless
They fall without permission
Doing what words fear to do
Drop from my tongue without permission
You taught me to fear my words
Fear my voice
Because I speak too loud for you?
Did I speak the truth?
Or it was easier if I was defenceless
Defenceless against you
Two took my voice
In very different ways
1 stole from me
2 beat me with her rage
You were the perfect team,
Oxygen, a spark
One of you hit a match one just breathed
Forest fires began to burn
You see,
I'm charred beyond recognition
So many things you burned
The voice you locked away
It works still okay
I'm still afraid of it today
As silent tears fall down my face
They speak for the voiceless
They speak for me
My voice doesn't know how to speak
This place got used to captivity
Shouting is a mystery

But my tears silently scream
The rage still in the cage
You built for my voice
I don't want to let it out
You think you have forest fires?
Lava flows underneath
Silent Tears

Kansas and Trauma

Tangled feet
My body hits the floor,
Tripping over memories
I've lived this life before
Shadows of the past
They grow around me
Whirling words and winds
Pain is back again
It never really leaves me
Whirlwinds and Tornados
Trauma
Every time steady legs feel firm,
You step into a sound
A glance, a voice, a gesture, or a word
You are back again
Like Dorothy transported to another world
Instead of colour,
Black and white
There is deadness here
Getting out of Kansas
Back to this moment in time
Fighting your way into your body
Back into your mind
You'll never understand the cyclone
Unless you've lived in fear

You'll never understand Kansas
Unless trauma lives in here
So if you find me someday
Fighting back to you
Just sit beside me
Until I'm right here too
In Oz,
The life I live today
Until Kansas fades away

Enveloped Inside

Envelope enclosed
My very heart and soul
I sealed myself inside
Signed it with my pride
Stamped with fear and shame
This envelope of me
Mailbox and a key
A way to hide inside
Never see the light
I thought it would be safe
Wouldn't be torn again
Pain couldn't break-in
Decay
Decay found me anyway
Until it hurt to stay this way
So I'm taking out my envelope
Returning my key,
I'm letting the safe ones see
Read the letter that is me
I wasn't meant to be a mystery

Here Am I

Here am I
Light, lighting my sky
Looks a like copper-covered night
Dark fire trying to hide
Here am I
Laden heavy
A being created for light
Created to know
Yet born to dark
Born to ripped hearts
Born to beasts
This darkness crippling me
Here am I
Grown full yet empty
Age-like lines on a tree
Reveal where I'm meant to be
Cut-out pieces show
Where wounds turned infectious
Here am I
Perception shift
Further than my darkness
Can you see what light created me to be
When interruptions jumped in

Here am I
Lightning moment
Can you see how far?

Now?
Rescued from the dark
Yet surrounded by it
Put my heart down
Slice me open
Filet me like a fish
I will choose this
Here am I
Separate me
Pull out the dark
Leave the light
Scars and broken bones
Trauma victim inside
Heal me open
Let me bleed
On this table
Let the light lead the way
Running to pain
Suffering deep
Here am I
Trying to get up
In a surgery
Just leads to more injury
So still will I lay
Here am I
In the hands that spoke my being
Into being
Knowing deep
Wisdom is His
I will follow
Here am I
O Here am I

Trees Trying to Breathe

Drenched with water
Trees I wander past
Alive in the deep black
I wonder what lives underneath
Wonder worlds that live with water
I will open up my chest
Cut myself open
Spread my ribs
So you can see my lungs
Drenched in water
Like the trees,
I'm just trying to breathe
I'll show you how thick
How the air forces its way
How a moment can send them
Pushing the air away
The danger of water so high
You can't see what's underneath
Come, I'll show you
The trauma that's in me
The way my brain works
It's always on a ledge
The first sign of danger
The instincts kick in

The numb hands or prickling
As my lungs move so fast
Rushing to get air in
The panic is settling in
Or you could see me slow
I'd just be small and still
Stay in place
Or these lungs you see could fill with oxygen so I could
Run and run and run

So see. it's not just in my head
I can show you underneath
The reactions you see
The trauma in me
It's not that it could happen
It's that it did happen again and again
If I crack myself open show, you my lungs,
Can you never again tell me to calm
Calm down
Telling me that doesn't help
Remind me where I am
Tell me to remind my lungs to breathe in and out again

Section 3

Pass Me Not - Fanny Crosby- Hymn

"1 Pass me not, O gentle Savior,Hear my humble cry,While on others Thou art calling,Do not pass me by.Refrain:Savior, Savior,Hear my humble cry;While on others Thou art calling,Do not pass me by.2 Let me at a throne of mercy,Find a sweet relief,;Kneeling there in deep contrition,Help my unbelief. [Refrain]3 Trusting only in Thy merit,Would I seek Thy face;Heal my wounded, broken spirit,Save me by Thy grace. [Refrain]4 Thou the Spring of all my comfort,More than life to me,Whom have I on earth beside Thee? Whom in heav'n but Thee? [Refrain]"

Abandoned Soul

My house still stands
Wood covering windows and doors
Abandoned house, abandoned soul
I've never been anywhere that cold
Where you could feel it
Feel it past your bone
And down into your marrow

Trapped within am I
Left to death and decay
I'm screaming, but indifference rises up
Dust and rust is all they can see
I'm trapped inside, yet my heart still beats

Don't you know what it's like to be left alone
To be always, always on your own
Everyday closer to a wreaking ball;
Somedays that seems like hope
Isolation breaks the strongest souls

I think that's what you meant
When you boarded me up inside
That I was weak and being weak, I would die
That loving them was not loving you
And so I had to pay

You boarded me up and left me here
They watched and looked away

I was a story
A story you could tell
The one who died inside
Who loved and was killed

You left me in isolation
Hoping I'd die quietly
I guess you were wrong
She still lives within me
And still, I breathe

Abandoned
Though I am
A Crowbar has broken in
Bringing air and light
Feeding me what love has known I need

I know, I know you thought you'd win
But, here this house still stands
And as the carpenter rebuilds
He comes and holds my hand
He tells me that though it stings
This is not the end

If I could tell you one thing
I would tell you this
Hurting me doesn't make you free
Speaking hate is way too easy

Buried Me

Excavate
Dig
Dig me up
Shovels digging deep
We've done this before
The grave robber and me

Archeology is not lost on me
You keep digging me up and planting me back
You're like an archaeologist digging up the same city
Every time you forget the ending

See, you buried me here
You stole me from the ground you placed over me
You resurrect ears and brain
You need them for listening
You need to be heard
Here we are again

I'm just a science experiment
How many times?
How many times can you bury me in
the dirt of your indifference?
Maybe a thousand
I'm not sure anymore
I can't keep score
You never let me rest
Let the indifference or hatred sink in

Let the looks of disgust do me in
You keep gouging me out
Burying and uncovering me again and again

Gravedigger, stop coming in need
Then burying me deeper in your revulsion for me
I'm not your conquered city
I gave my love freely

Now just let me rest in the realm of the dead
Where I'm no longer a science experiment
Parts of me on sale for free
The parts of me you think you need

For a moment
Then disgust rises up
You bury me again
Until you need something from me

If you come again
Look where you think you left me
I'm not in the ground
Not buried alive by abuse and disgust
So don't look for me in the dust

Buried me
Is extinct

Section 4

Come You, Disconsolate- Thomas Moore and Thomas Hastings - Hymn

"1 Come, you disconsolate, where'er you languish;come to the mercy seat, fervently kneel.Here bring your wounded hearts, here tell your anguish;earth has no sorrows that heaven cannot heal.2 Joy of the desolate, light of the straying,hope of the penitent, fadeless and pure!Here speaks the Comforter, in mercy saying,"Earth has no sorrows that heaven cannot cure."3 Here see the bread of life; see waters flowing forth from the throne of God, pure from above.Come to the feast prepared; come, ever knowing earth has no sorrows but heaven can remove."

Sea of Misery

Set out to sea in misery
On the waves of pain
Hoping my small frame
Can keep the deep underneath me
Withstand the undercurrents
Pulling me to and fro
I'm not sure where to go
Oh Body, my body, just keep me afloat
Don't let me sink
The pain is building like waves
All at once, crashing into the shore
I'm trying to tell the storm
Quiet
But it gets louder in my ears
Waves demanding to be felt
Currents pulling me down
My body weightless finished fighting the relentless pain
I'm out to sea in misery
Can anyone see
My pain unspoken is drowning me

Cold Floor

Laying on the cold floor
Smashed insides
Shaking body heaving
You walk back in
Saying how much you love me
If I could only get it right
It's for my own good, you say
Reeling me in with words I've always wanted to hear
You expect the words you say will fix everything
But all they do is make you feel better
and keep me hanging on
"It's not always bad"
"I was stupid "
"It's my fault"
Trying to shake my insides back together,
Trying to make sense of something senseless
But truth is, truth was
Smashed girl is not so easily fixed
Broken pieces are not so easily put back together

Section 5

Day by Day- Caroline W. Sandell Berg- Hymn

"1 Day by day and with each passing moment,Strength I find to meet my trials here;Trusting in my Father's wise bestowment,I've no cause for worry or for fear.He whose heart is kind beyond all measure Gives unto each day what he deems best—Lovingly, its part of pain and pleasure,Mingling toil with peace and rest.2 Ev'ry day the Lord himself is near me,With a special mercy for each hour;All my cares he gladly bears and cheers me,He whose name is Counselor and Pow'r.The protection of his child and treasure Is a charge that on himself he laid:"As your days, your strength shall be in measure"—This the pledge to me he made.3 Help me then in ev'ry tribulationSo to trust your promises, O Lord,That I lose not faith's sweet consolationOffered me within your holy Word.Help me, Lord, when, toil and trouble meeting,E'er to take, as from a father's hand,One by one, the days, the moments fleeting,Till I reach the promised land."

Never Seen!

I've seen many things in this wide old world
Many things I'd rather forget
Pain, an abyss of pain trying to swallow
a good friend whole
Seen people die without ever turning to the Lord
Seen cruelty and lived under its feet

Seen pulpits filled with the dead speaking to those who live
Seen babies discarded like garbage without
a thought or a care
Seen samaritans turned into monsters
by just one word in the air

Oh, I've seen many things I'd rather not see again
Seen friends turned into strangers without a word
Seen fathers turned into memories ashes of who they were
Seen despair take a gentle soul burying its own body deep

But one thing I've never seen
I've never seen the righteous forsaken,
Never seen the Lord's chosen rejected
Pain will come to us all

But the promise of God!
Not lightly made
He will fulfil his every word
Not one of his promises fail to return
No not one will return void

Every promise, every word
Full to overflowing, many with tears

Looking back through the years
The times we thought he lied to our ears
Reminding each other when the darkness descends
We have never seen the righteous forsaken
His promises remain

If you've lost your way I'll tell you again
The Lord has never forsaken you
He won't start today
We'll remind each other today
We have never seen the righteous forsaken

No matter what we see
No matter what we live
No matter how it hurts to breathe
We have never seen the righteous forsaken
We are held and sustained
Always safe in his hands
We remain

New Skin

Lord you are
Peeling off my skin
Until I can grow new again
Skin, not scales or scars
Not barbed wire around my heart
Skin that isn't so broken
Skin that isn't infected
Skin that isn't gaping open wounds
Peeling off all that skin
I'm naked flesh
Hover over me, Lord
Cover me with your wings
Protect me from the evil one
All those sent to maim me
Until I have new skin
Skin that isn't so thin
Skin that isn't so marred
New Skin
And maybe a new heart

Ocean of Words

The words sit stuck in my throat
Begging me to open my mouth, let them come out
My mind yells
Tell them what you think
This is your chance
Your moment
Ask
Knock
Say it

But then the words turn to dust in my lungs
All those speeches you gave me about
How anything I had to say was
Inconvenient
Stupid
Foolish
Burdensome

Until all my words turned to sand
The waters of who I am drying up
Scorched by your rages
Until I looked more like desert
Than ocean

All those beautiful creatures I was meant to name
All those pearls of value strung together poetry
Had to die in the harshness of your sun
All it would have taken for ocean to come to life

Water words of blessing, not of cursing,
But you didn't, did you?
Had more cursing than any life should,
But I know the one who gave me words
He put them within me
All that roaring sea
I must use it wisely
Be a blessing

But someday, you will see
The ocean pouring out of me
You won't be able to dry it up
Living water

Someday those words will spill out
All that harm and hesitation
Will be a minor memory
Of when my voice was taken from me

Afterword

"Ah, Sovereign Lord, you have made the heavens and the earth by your great power and outstretched arm.Nothing is too hard for you." Jeremiah 32:17

Natasha Roblin

Natasha Roblin is the author of Soul Perch: A collection of poems. Natasha began writing poetry many years ago as an outlet. Natasha always says the words belong to the Lord; He gives them to me. Natasha lives in Ontario, Canada. You can contact her at soulperchbook@hotmail.com or https://www.facebook.com/soulperchbook. 

www.ingramcontent.com/pod-product-compliance
Lightning Source LLC
Chambersburg PA
CBHW011943050726
47590CB00011B/3341